THE NOTEBOOK
FEARLESS FEELINGS

unadultered virgin thoughts buckled together to ruffle a few feathers

FAHEEM IQBAL SHAYIQ

First Published in February 2021

ISBN: 978-93-5427-555-5

BLUEROSE PUBLISHERS
www.bluerosepublishers.com
info@bluerosepublishers.com
+91 8882 898 898

Cover Design:
Riya

Typographic Design:
Namrata Saini

Distributed by: BlueRose, Amazon, Flipkart, Shopclues

To all dedicated foes whose constant fiddle expiated sins shaping me into a better human being.

"I don't wish to be clad with an artificial authority, if it robs off my inherent humanness"

Acknowledgement

All praise to Allah, the almighty, the lord of this universe !

Whatever little I could achieve in my life has been purely an outcome of the blessings of my beloved parents, Prof.(Retd.) Fatah Mohd Shayiq & Rafiqa Shayiq, who left no stones unturned to see me grow & see me through. I consider myself very lucky for being brought up in pleasant environs courtesy my beloved parents.

I have been very attached to my siblings & amongst them all Er. Sajad holds a very special place. A gifted talent gone waste, who is in the middle of a prolonged fight with life. I wish him a speedy recovery. Asif Shayiq (LL.M, M.A), is the youngest & the brightest of the lot. I wish him best of luck in his endeavours. Tasneem Kouser, a teacher by profession & at home has truly lived up to the expectations being the senior. I wish her & the lovely kids, Farhan & Arhan, a life full of joy.

Another special child deserving mention here is our sweetheart Dua, the daughter of Sajad & Rehana. All love & prayers for her & her parents.

I can't afford to ignore a person who has stood behind me like a rock in every thick & thin& held things together for me. She has never let me down & instead gone a step ahead as far as my expectations from her. Tahira Hussain has really sacrificed a lot. I shall always love her no matter what !

Last but not the least, my beautiful daughters, Hoor, Haniya & Hadiya along with the little champ Imran, make my life complete. My God bless them with a long & prosperous life.

Finally I thank Blue Rose Publications for bringing up this publication in time.

Faheem Iqbal Shayiq,

B.Sc, M.A (Eng), LL.M(Constitutional Law), N.E.T (Law)

Associate Executive, J&K Bank

Contents:

Heart of a father

The light in the dark is the heart of a father

A lively spark is the heart of a father

The love of this lord is never flawed

Noah's ark is the heart of a father

Endures pain yet never complains

Such gracious remark is the heart of a father

In despair deluge, you taketh refuge

The tranquil landmark is the heart of the father

Knows, shows, vows with little remorse

A kind monarch is the heart of the father

Chapter I

Life Algebra:

Enduring the flirt of destiny

She plays games, I ready a game plan

She brags on running writs

I keep cajoling my dying spirits

To her offers of endless sorrow

I keep accepting with such firm resolve,

That I shall overcome every now & then

No matter which way, where & when

She evinces carrying the absolute will

In defiance I offer my only skill

To sustain & survive amidst this belief

Of my attempts to delay the inevitable grief

Life was no bed of roses, but a mesh of thorns, so craftily woven into an apparent rosary. Amidst this, your luck is a rare hand pluck. A sane man had already foretold the truth, summing the whole as one nasty, short & brute phenomenon. This shortness of tenure makes you gasp for your breath. And at times, it turns into a wild galloping horse. The swirls it takes exacts from you a firm grip on your holds to remain saddled & collect your quantum of solace on this adventure embark. As you peddle on the majorly bumpy roads, on every step you take & every move you make, your perseverance shall be put to test. But you must have your share of greener pastures on this mostly rough entourage.

Go gather ye rose buds!

Keep the rivers of belief flowing, in rain & sun alike till you straddle onto the imagined shores. Keep afloat & don't drown.

Keep Doing Good:

It cometh naturally unless you stir some sort of a rebellion within. The 'good', must ostensibly come without expecting equal good. In a real life scenario, mathematical niceties are thrown over the precipice. Life is more about assumptions, presumptions, expectations, or hope, which sustains your balance even being on a tight or for that matter at the end of the rope. Here life can throw such unimaginable complexities. A one plus one, could make it eleven, or for that matter may throw up a miraculous gain or relegate to an unfathomable loss & such gainsay. So forget doing good shall guarantee a return of proportionate equal good. The moment you rid yourself from such a pull, the more you shall fall in line & in turn be just fine!

Let your imagination act an all weather companion!

Turn imagination upside down

Have frozen treats by the sky

Be up in letting every other thing frown

If come you agree,

Over the greens & beneath the blues,

Ruffle your feathers & just fly higher

Through the beaming gleam, feel the kiss of air

Break the shackles that hold your desire

& fill in your cup on the joys held higher

as if caged now set free

Gleefully we shall escape out of here

& flee into the heavens!!!

Keep Trying Your Best:

Do your best & forget about the rest. The best use is of your own resource & recourse. For if you succeed, done & fun. Even if you fail, you still won't feel that numb & frail. A sure shot in this case is you shrug off from yourself any blame paradigm that could otherwise weigh you down. Contrarily if you fail to explore yourself, you chance into degeneracy of the worst kind & only rot your soul. Discover yourself who you are, at the first place & should you lose track keep rediscovering to keep you steady on the sails & keep your tail up.

Live the horse attitude...

The stables housing the warriors

Let loose to run over the barriers

Trained to conquer, the diktat so loud

Resounding through the hostile crowd

The royal horses are out with a vow

To assume the throne & deal a blow

To fetters holding their tread to glory

& critics who jump the gun in hurry

The whispering tornado on their torso

Unpack the gunpowder in their ammo

To lit up hellfire from fuelled desire

The moment the war trumpet is blown

When the stage is set & dice is thrown

& as the bolts undrew, speed echoes

God speed! Through columns & rows

Behind the enemy lines unfurl the flag

Empty unto them the gallop drag !!!

Reach self- sufficiency, earlier the better:

Easy said than done. But there is no harm practising. If we go by maths, self sufficiency is inversely proportional to your needs. The more of them means an over reliance on others. And learn to differentiate needs from necessities. Your bread & butter is your necessity. You grasp your necessity no matter what. But then needs can go on & on, till you find yourself struggling through a jigsaw. You may wish to have everything & yearn to posses. But if you don't, you still are better off. The question determining which course you take, is your likening for the better off or going far off & in the process risk going off balance!

On all your tempt attempt, keep an eye on the contempt you may commit.

Lay bare this tryst such blunt desire

Immersion to embark & fiddle with fire

This notoriety peaking in such hazy days

When every soul braves this thrown open maze

This contemptuous tempt to rid the forbearance

Not heeding to what the wise foretold

Of sacred muses meant to behold

To stay clear & eschew the utterance

Boiling like hell, forcing the vents, hence

This flagrant delving of kept rendezvous

Doubt this retrogressiveness sustain

This bewildering cacophonous refrain

Then may augment through coerce

Or better prune this vile & mere otiose !

Trusted Lieutenants-

Since the ride is more dilly dally than any roller coaster. A semblance of rescue is discernible from a few rare souls. Stick to this lot & don't get swayed into every sympathetic shouldering. A mere pat may be just an attempt to keep you charmed in good humour. Mostly people & at most of the times, shall draw a sadistic pleasure out of your sufferings. You are here to fight your own battle. An external succourer from a well to do source at times of need but no to every invading tom, dick & harry. Your composure during any turbulence shall actually define your persona. Master this craft. Over reliance shall chance you getting belittled & it shall haunt at the worst juncture no matter what class you wear on your sleeve.

Don't Tell, Don't Yell, Just Dwell In Your Own Little Space!

I don't tell, when I was hurt

I don't yell even in a spurt!

I don't revel on them being in trouble

I don't dwell in their random flirt

I don't tell them to let'em bubble

I don't spell their filth & dirt

I don't bell their rings even subtle

I don't settle the requisite scores

I don't battle for'em to belittle

I don't swell their ripened sores

I don't peddle like'em their lies

I don't sell lows, neither my highs!

I don't rebel now for a reason, but then

I don't travel endlessly unison!!!

Naturally from this follows another paradigm, why be too docile when you fought alone all this while?

Don't be more loyal than the dog. Your master shall always & for sure manipulate you for his own end. You must not in the false pretext of featuring in their good books, ruin your own pages. Yes don't over exert. Every appreciation from a master must be seen a dubious design of exploit in the hindsight. Of course you must do your duty, to avoid getting reduced to some meddlesome interloper or becoming just one useless crap. Just do the part of your stuff & call out the bluff!

Friends & Clients Are Distinguishable:

Clients & friends are not going to fit in one equation. One shall surely force the other out of the equation. Certainly depending on a tending inquisition, you either act in grace with your best pals & in business don't mind the disgrace. If a person, conceives a win-win thing exclusively for his own person, be clear you are not in the company of a friend. At the best, you are in business. The defining moment is the person's timing of approach & desert !

Be only luke-warm:

Don't pamper people, no matter who, so much so, that you fail to comprehend the amount of warmth you must dissipate. An underserved warm attitude could even embolden a minion at your own cost, propel his confidence to make him nurse an altogether different feel. To your disadvantage, his self-confidence will skyrocket over a period & you definitely would run the risk of being taken for granted or even for a ride.

So keep an eye! & don't complain why later!!

To a nonchalant flutter in wings

Oft doth fail me my trivial things

Of men so obtruse, women so servile

In a wasteland that appears fertile

They put up brave faces of queens & kings

They crave for the glam, from shreds of shame

In their quests, they're all the same

Running for charm so preposterous

All random chores, crouches & cringes

Makes'em early to cook up a tale

But leave their trail in random stirrings

They feed on my calm without a fail

I drown my qualms in mystic springs

Play to win: Be the eventual winner

In the recorded history, hardly shall you come across a struggle that fell on its face. No matter how hard the toil & quest, it will sooner or later boil down to a graceful victory. Rest assured, the ordeal will be no deal, should you have your eyes set on the prize. All your luck is lying in arrears & this shall pay back its worth in full measures. Don't just rust your weaponry. Keep sharpening your blades & redefining your arsenal. On just a round at the corner, lies your destiny. One more stride & you are all caught up. One last rep to reminding yourself before any change of heart appears to build up. The fact is you started & there is a connected fact WHY?

So Hold on! The triumph & glory is just awaiting you on the other side.

And we must be readying our victory parade...

This slothful embrace will only rot your soul

Cajole your spirit, brace up for the role

Unless you chance yourself, unto your own explore

Don't be this unjust, to the part of your whole

Your cribs n confines, won't let you intertwine

Will only make you stink, & never make you shine

You gotta pump some blood & let out that noise

You oughta bring that kick, to ooze out some poise

This must just augur well, I need to foretell

You maybe doing fine but be the probable,

Who maketh possible, that you see in you!

Give up the falsity & make it count true!!

The beauty you behold needs be loud told

Till the shimmer faketh, until it abounds gold

Just hang on to belief, recline not in grief,

For the ensuing joy, will sure sink in deep

& set you on your course to what you did endorse

For when you do embark, you better the remorse

So you must now hasten to this quest call

Heads held high & let the walk be tall

I am on await, on the other side with glee

To see you donning grace & embracing victory!

Chapter II

A Retreat To The Dark Age:

Defeaning cries & desperate moans

On a piece of land that nobody owns

Many a random gang claim the spoils

In absence of peers, hardly any toils

They seem to walk with gifts on a platter

In this boring, flip flop theatre

Bereft of defiant & resolute men

Bereft of any prowess or conviction

Hopeless case the whole rank & file

Who busied doing nothing all this while

& to no astound caught off guard

Ostensibly inviting the wrath of God

False tall claims & fat true lies

Ugly lecturing grace, cartoons donning ties

Competing within themselves these despo fools

Praise to Lord, God, Almighty, for bestowing men with some reason. The creator would usually ordain to exact from this blessed creation a reasoned application of mind to advance a sustainable conclusion. Pitily in today's age, an elusive alternate phenomenon is garnering plenitude attention & eventually an unfortunate acceptance. The constant fiddle with natural instincts is a deliberate nourish machination aimed at creating an unassailable gap to realism. The rationale steadily gets subordinated to abounden creativity, unabated sensationalism & myopic fanaticism reproducing more ideologues than sane men. In the contemporary times, this phenomenon has received an unparalleled & unprecedented patronage. This has consumed a huge populace, owing largely to an aggressive indoctrination, facilitated by a vigorous propaganda machine. The reprehensible random, benighted lobby, which sprang to life, post a hideous, debatable power grab & in their pursuit of hatched agenda, sources this toxic indoctrination, & a dedicated propaganda machine takes it to another level. To foreclose any remote chances of revival of some rationalistic outpour, the hired men, travel an extra mile in their holy pursuit of manufacturing lies. In this dark fashion, the so called fourth pillar of democracy has receded with a severest hit to be reduced to an incredible hall of shame. A self proclaimed illuminati armed with hypnotic graphic content appear on prime time to bulldoze any rationale. A resistant minority of well travelled & polished men, women, capable of reviving reason, are tactfully put through a harsh smear campaign. A powerful weapon, uniquely conceived through a rephrased notion of "Nationlality", quite different to what a man of normal prudence would understand it. The residue is weighed down out of the scheme into non relevance after failing to fit in this new definition & the unsatisfied jury at the media trial holds this miniscule minority guilty. This sense of imposed guilt forces them into silence & haunts the rest audience, leaving the actual victim an easy meat to be fed to the untamed predators. Sequentially served narrative is emptied into such awaiting fine receptacles. This committed lot then loses no time to practise what was propounded by this illegal theory. A viral opinion is manufactured (a misconceived modern day 'volks-geist' or the will of majority) providing the much intended fuel for the vicious cycle to operate. Combat mentality gets superimposed & the result is obvious. The media instead of shedding some light becomes a tour guide into the world taken over by darkness & an accomplice to what ensues.

CHRONOLOGY OF LOSS & GAIN

Chapter III

An Unending Quest:
For That Ideal Teacher

Teacher possesses the skill to transform an ignorant lot into an enlightened one. Although this enlightenment doesn't always come that easy. The quantum of toil is proportional to the fertility of the brains of the subject. The teacher, as such, at a basic or primary level has a job at hand & its sincere implementation goes a long way in shaping the virgin brains. This stage usually receives incidental favours, like the keen interest of the guardian to ensure his ward getting the right amount of attention & treatment. The accountability graph on teacher acquires its peak at this stage. A fairly balanced approach sees the child through to dream of a flourishing career as per his tending orientation.

The student consequently slips into a college or varsity. At this stage, the teacher's role attains more significance for a plethora of reasons. One important aspect is the slowly dwindling accountability owing to many factors like, the student being taken for granted by teachers & guardians all alike. Nevertheless the teacher under all circumstances is capable to further shape & polish the faculties of students, so that his credentials sell like hot cakes in an operative market. Here the teacher's matured response is key & plays a pivotal role in lifting the morale of his taught. The copper smith can be harsh at his subject but an ornamentalist can ill afford to take any chances & in the process make mistakes. The teacher at the higher level of study is akin to an ornamentalist. Higher the level of study, judicious is the expected approach. A fairly balanced approach must in all cases ensure the subject to come up to the expectations.

Albeit! We rarely come across a scenario were teacher appears to have chosen the avocation with the sought purpose. The higher we go, the cooler we tend to get. A disastrous lack in commitment sets in, marauds the moral & ethical fabric of our educational system. With the entrustment, the teacher turns into a monster & whatever authority he is delegated with turns him into a sheer authoritarian, instead of turning him a trustee. He starts to play foul. To this the society plays fool & the ridicule continues.

He puts on a biased glass & his peeps through such spectacles are the eventual source of debacle. He differentiates the blue eyed from the rest. The lesser children of god receive little encouragement & recede to the hindsight to leave the ground open for nepotism to take its first firm roots. Even a dedicated teacher in such overwhelmed scheme falters due to alienation. The psychological aspect at this stage has a direct bearing on the future of the taught. Even a scratch at it ripens into a sore & carries drastic implications. Nepotism does truly promote inefficiency but it also gives birth to demoralised men, who later fail to explore their fullest & remain half baked for life. This dis-service to the society must in all cases have its cascading effect. For a duty towards society is a duty towards God.

And anything that goes against the divine system is worthy of wrath.

Beyond the first teacher I had in my father

I really don't care, neither do I bother

To address a whole many monsters as teachers

Who chose the avocation & not the spirit

Whose hirings even, are a long kept secret

To be reduced to mere fixtures

In the faculty who consume & excrete

So scandalously selective &discreet

Their to accentuate & not assuage

They may still rise by virtue of a camouflage

In this still age what progressive stage?

Let's then only pray to God & heaven,

Safer passage & long life for the children

Chapter IV

A Motivated Examiner (One From the Jew Lobby)

Examination occupies a central position in our educational system. Examination scheme influences classroom practices to a large extent as the classroom practices are considered to be a means to an end. Unfortunately largely this phrase gets misconceived & misinterpreted. It does not achieve the real objective of the curriculum. The trend of appearing in exams for the mere sake of obtaining a degree, diploma, or a certificate becomes the sole purpose of educational activities in our educational institutions. There is a need to improve the teaching learning processes in our educational system. The exams should be patterned to assess the students in developmental terms. The examination pattern needs to take into account all the processes & products consistently in accordance with the aims & objectives of education. The aim can be illustrated by the phrase, 'education is the modification of behaviour'. The behavioural modification has to be in positive terms & the process of learning is supposed to civilize the taught apart from & in addition to the usual service of literacy. The exams must gauge whether the individual is on the right course. The notion of qualified graduates taking up professions like medicine, engineering or law is good but the success of the educator lies in returning civilized citizenry back in the social milieu, enthused with a vision & a mission & in tune with the utilitarian philosophy. In order to reach this avowed objective, we need to facilitate change within the system, including of course the reformation in examination patterns. The National Education Policy, 1986, also highlighted the credibility of exams has lessened. Examination has three main aspects, viz., the academic, administrative & evaluative. Any reform in the system needs a concomitant reform in all these aspects. An effective examination system must have the characteristics like detailed syllabi, indicating there in the aims & objectives, skills & proficiencies etc.

It has been found that syllabi are usually vaguely drafted & obsolete things repeated. The paper-setters, moderators, & examiners must be trained keeping these objectives in consideration. Question papers should be based on blue-prints & design indicating weightage to instructional objectives. In contrast to all that can be said, it is not uncommon in our state that students complain about being asked out of box questions, a common term in vogue in the state. Even the students at the post graduate level feel let down in an examination, by virtue of many reasons. For example some complain that there papers get evaluated by even their senior students, or teachers having no specialization in that particular stream, which in turn suggests no competence in the activity being undertaken. At times it is taken to another level, with a single teacher evaluating more than one subject, irrespective of his/her expertise in the concerned subject. A university teacher in the examination department, on anonymity, reflected that the university professors who draw huge salaries show little interest in evaluating papers as this process doesn't promise them bounties. They consider it wastage of time. Thus in the process of finding alternatives, they end up assigning the same to evaluators eager to take up the assignment. There have been glaring instances of fraud reported, wherein the teacher, delegates such important function, to associates, research students working under them, having no regard to the fact that they are actually evaluating papers of their future competitors. This compromise is perpetuated with impunity & was witnessed when at the law department research level exams, a senior student, working under the supervision of the teacher concerned, was authorised to evaluate & mark papers. How can one expect fair play under such a vague scheme of things. This shows the wilful disregard of their duties on the part of the so called teachers. The system of both internal as well external exams must be transparent & students who are not convinced, having every right to be not, under such hostile circumstances, must be allowed to re-evaluate their scripts. But then the thief usually knows what he has stolen & tries every method to conceal it. Much akin to this, the evaluators, for reasons better known to them, though obvious to people who have the understanding, write long negative remarks in order to foreclose any option at the re evaluation stage, to force his judgement on the re-evaluator. Writing notes & remarks is akin to taking away the whole thing which is offered by the provision, reducing its efficacy to a naught. So instead of getting mistakes, if any, cured, the evaluator forces his judgement on the person re-evaluating & usually the re examiner is made to form a poor opinion at the outset.

A victim of this very devilish act, a student, who was sure shot of fetching more grades than were allotted to him under this vested scheme, applied for a re-evaluation. By the time the revision was announced, he sought a copy of the answer script through RTI. He was astonished to find out longer notes than the answers itself after every answer, trying to justify lesser grades given, as if the teacher was sure of somebody shall try to find out what has gone wrong. The student had already understood what the fate of re evaluation was going to be like. This bizarre mechanism is placed at an apex body, boasting of regulating the system. We can only laugh this absurdity off.

Chapter V

One Skewed Playfield:

Frauds and scams are not uncommon in any civilization, irrespective of its stage of development. The perpetrators of these frauds mostly in earlier times took advantage of the lesser avenues of discovery. The enlightenment struck a death blow to this trade in the dark. As the phrase would best explain this thesis, "sunlight is the best disinfectant", the light of awareness brought more and more frauds to surface and the authorities were able to formulate strict rules to censure. Whilst the civilization keeps innovating mechanisms to check abuse, abusers cross check the mechanism and innovate. This tussle leads to chicken-egg causation and the cycle goes on. University of Kashmir can serve as a beautiful example. Nobody will deny its ornamental value, given its large, lush green and carefully maintained campus. But that is all it offers.

The soul ought to have been as beautiful as the face! For having a case in place.

From my personal experience it can without exaggeration be stated, its soul has been rotten and what the picturesque scene offers is all that it has. This assertion portrays a sorry figure which may not be necessarily taken as a dispassionate viewpoint. Having remained in the campus for almost six years, the only thing that captivated my mind and soul was its serene environs. Behind the veil of this attractive enshroud lies a dismal, ugly and dirty picture.

The bias and prejudice starts right from the day of entry to this august school of learning.

On the very first day you start discovering a visible divide, the birds with the same feather flocking together and all of a sudden, you start getting conscious of your tread. The gross manipulation of results by virtue of fathers, godfathers to try and ensure the continued possession of this piece of property is the next priority. Well this is very tactfully done by first creating an aura in the faculty that his or her ward is a walking 'encyclopaedia' even prior to receiving his or her first lecture of enlightenment. The spectacles through which the teacher peeps converge at the same blessed child with an engaging smile notwithstanding his Lombrosian gaze at the rest. Eventually semesters are passed, the 'special taught' gets rescued from lagging behind by a quick internal assessment succourer. They can easily get his PhD awarded but what about the encyclopaedia thing. They can't prove themselves wrong! Foresight really! So the marks in the assessment justify their averment.

The rest have to ingest whatever residual blessing could be afforded after satisfying the sacred wishes, the collective conscience of the faculty. Now all this is done actually to retain this gifted intellect after his very careful grooming and well managed studies.

Alas! The wish mostly fails.

Some among the horribly treated lot survive the campus scourge and manage to gather more scoring points after venturing out of the serene environs, quite a contrast though, than the blessed damozel during hiring process, courtesy these saviour UGC regulations. Now the regulations give some a real headache given the desperation that their projected 'encyclopaedia' must in all cases end up in the library. The collective conscience of the faculty in all cases has to be satisfied. So they sit around, introspect and work out a plan – issue an advert, shortlist the eligible, call them for interview and create a scene of serious hiring process. But inside the four walls they have nobody but themselves to execute their dubious and nefarious plans.

They have the guts to manage a special Skype interview for a privileged child, what a level playing field comparing those who are asked to be present in person before the learned panel at the interview well before the scheduled time, with directions of producing original documents. You cannot raise an objection to this discrimination and why should you, how much leverage the person will get by appearing on Skype.

At the most he or she could keep one Google tab open whilst making the august presence felt. Even there is no requirement in such a case for verifying the originals. They have the audacity to openly flout UGC norms by getting another blue eyed baby in on the premise of convincing them in a space of two minutes notwithstanding the fact that his academic merit is far behind than the other aspirants despite all the blessings and pleasantries, even not bothering the caveat that interview carries only 20 percent weightage as per UGC guidelines.

Besides there is indeed no necessity of quorum as required by UGC in such special cases but yes they cover this fraud quite artistically. They call the selectees by phone, ask them to collect their appointment letters, sans the final list, sans the total tally of points, sans everything.

The interview is actually a cosmetic fraud in the garb of which a game of making or breaking of careers is

played. The dirty picture concludes with a sigh!

The worthy selectees are quietly made to join and one fine day you get to know about the appointments. On that day the only question left unanswered is when and how the selection process was completed.

You walk your ways, they walk theirs.

Masked mediocrity tasked to reign

No strings attached of stooping so mean

From the dirt & dust you demon derive

Then why must you to a logic arrive

For so overwhelming doses of gracious giveaways

To shut struck others, to guide them through ways

Unknown! For the hegemony has to thrive

& afford their ward to safely arrive

Riding on injustice so unfathomable & severe

They conceive so effortlessly this obvious design

How so revealing their dirty align

For the sweat doesn't drip from those ugly foreheads

Whilst they rip dreams & the dungeon feeds

Upon the deserving yet helpless child of god

Yet nobody to comprehend & read out them loud

HOBSONS CHOICES

Chapter VI

Banking Job: A Honey Trap of Another Kind

There is a phrase, 'Hobson's Choice', tracing its origin to a livery stable owner in Cambridge, England.

Thomas Hobson, The owner was so astute in his trade flourish, that he would trick his clients into buying even those horses, which would otherwise find less takers. In his stall, he offered customers the choice of either taking the horse bound nearest to the door or taking none at all. So no points for guessing what stuff would feature nearest to the door!

In our society, there is a race in time to just latch on to an exciting avocation. An avocation of your choosing.

But seldom do you find a would be lawyer donning an apron & a worthy doctor doing the medicine! A man spends half of his life honing a skill only to end up pursuing something beyond his will. Still does he continue to making a living but hardly does he live. Forgive me for the sin that I may myself be accused of committing. Owing to a factored miscalculation notwithstanding & of course some real bad luck.

A circumstantial trigger may just prompt a thinking man to just do the unthinkable. Let that sink in. We are just makers of our destiny and yet we call it fate, as Benjamin Desraile argues. So of the abundant trades to play with in this universe, I consider banking the most ruthless thing that could happen to a reckless man. A honey trap of another kind! The Promising handsome pay-outs allure you into preoccupations, nursing the feel that a banker is one white collared executive living a dream job. However there is more to it than meets the naked eye. I will take a sigh! While I unhesitantly walk you through to familiarise with the reality surrounding a bank employee.

But before doing that, I shall make an attempt to do a bit of classification.

a. The Freebies For Freezies

(Freezies Here Mean The Frozen)

Forget weak men with serious insecurity traits. They will find pleasure in easy breakthroughs. More so when the ensuing task is no more than a mere physical exercise. For a physical exercise void of any mental entice fills the cup just about full for the seekers. For this group of deadwood, banking is one perfect safe refuge. For the avocation does never test your grey matter. An entrusted machine will jus be fine to make even numb hands play. Rest relaxed, the machine will guide you through every task you are supposed to accomplish. The role is more labourly than involving any creativity. This jolly lot seldom complains, even if the physical exercise is enforced unabated. Any manoeuvres by these committed men & women will foreclose their survival chances in an open game.

b.   Transit-Campers:

(A Nap Before Embarking To Wake Up Again)

The Transit-Campers must in all cases refrain from entering The avocation in the hope of an early exit. Whilst outside you are free to plan your moves, but once you chance yourself in, the door behind is struck shut, most of the times. A misconceived endeavour of sustaining balance for a while & as the dust settles, reconsidering their real business, doesn't work here. But to encourage those stuck on the highway, a quote will do just fine. 'A consistent man believes in destiny & a capricious man in chance'. Chance offenders are a marked contrast. If you are consistent in enduring a lot of pain, while you long for your destiny, you may still find an exit by slamming the shut door open, albeit! That may ask for more than just another sacrifice.

c.   Circumstantial Victims

(Being Offered Something In Absence Of Anything Else)

There is still another group of men, who despite their perseverance, eventually yield into accepting anything, when there is scope for nothing else. This is the worst group of victims donning a role which was alien to their character & slowly this role gets so superimposed, taking over the pitiable man, only to reduce him into a tool in the toolkit, always restraining his poise to be a self propelled full fledged machine. And steadily the scheme makes him learn to live with what he is actually doing now.

Not being a standalone saint, I myself chanced into the degeneracy of the worst kind & did a great disservice to my pitiable soul.

For a record, I never loved doing maths or for that matter even statistics. I was to play with words than fiddle with unknown herds.

In 2012, while I was writing my LL.M thesis, aspiring to teach at the university someday (though I would love to teach, & yet actually had begun to hate most of the teachers. For I had already discovered more arm-chair intellectuals than role models, more biased spectacles with diverging outlook than sympathetic gazes converging at you, more noise than polished statements, more jealous creatures than sane men in them. I still considered this an immediate source to my beloved avocation, ('still seek more knowledge to explore more potential & yet make a humble livelihood), but while I was on course, a Life changing event took place!

A result news notification popped on my laptop, reading out 'J&K Bank Announces Result of 'Relationship Executive' Written Test'. The name of the post itself is so alluring that a man of ordinary prudence just can't help falling prey & gets just swayed. Yet honestly the only curiosity was to qualify it as a part of a process I had undertaken. Even the appearance in the exam was forced unto me sometime back, when in the Kashmir University law library itself, a very revered senior, Mr. Khursheed Ahmad Bhat (who ironically ended up as a banker too), motivated me to appear in the exams, reading out the perks that the job promised. On his insistence, I filled the application form on the deadline date & probably he managed the fee on my behalf, since, I would usually run dry at the most needed time.

So, on a lighter note, my dear brother is actually guilty on two counts. I casually punched my roll number into the tab & was greeted with a 'Qualified For The Interview' message. A bit of a teenage celebration & I was on course to just focussing on the avowed objective.

By the time, the interview was done, we were pass outs & all set to explore the new maze waiting to be thrown at us. Whilst the interview at the bank saw all the LL.M pass outs (around 10 or so in number) qualifying & getting recruited, I still kept searching for the other avenues, which weren't forthcoming though. A notification for contractual engagement at central university was meanwhile out & looking at the shortlist, I stood a fair chance to get through & do what I was supposed to do. But with my family already convinced that I had got a desired job, my Dad decisively smacked any resistance to join. His interesting supposition that the present offer is better in terms of job security than I was opting for in the contractual capacity, would actually go on to convince an innocent soul like me, desperate for a breakthrough.

Though I still considered it a temporary halt & let myself in.

The 'Temporary' could get this 'Contemporary', has cluelessly inculcated some degree of pessimism. Still unable to come to terms with myself to what actually has been going on. Forget any interest, I was now preparing my mind to work at a place as employee, which I had never visited as a client even.

Now What I Perceived Myself To Be Doing-

On the first day of my office, I wore the best available attire, selecting a matching tie & accessories to look presentable, charmed more in the hindsight by the misconceived feel of being appointed in the officer cadre & must be doing the job ordained for an officer in common parlance. As I entered an alien territory (J&K Bank Handwara Main) along with another selectee, Mr. Ibrahim, I got the first-hand experience with herds of men, women moving hither thither, swarming like bees inside an otherwise organised looking space. A large spread hall, with two long rows of chairs & tables arranged opposite to each other, with officials gasping for a breather amidst an overtly engaging clientele, a comparatively smaller cabin followed, housing three to four officials doing the advance stuff but more organised with some semblance of peace as compared to the large noisy hall, adjacent to the of course well to do branch head cabin.

My gaze engaged me on the sight of two small empty cabins. I contemplated the two empty cabins were meant for the two of us to work, with possibly a support staff to make us feel more at home.

What It Turned Out To Be-

But sooner I began to realise, all was not going to be as rosy as was conceived. The two of us entered the branch head cabin with our appointment letters. After a very brief intro, the branch head lost no time to whisk us away to that savagely busy hall. The first misconception of having an independent & private space was busted forthwith. We got our share of a chair & a table apiece, on those long rows & were left to fend for ourselves.

And with the passage of time sans any formal induction training, we learnt to do our part of the stuff on those newly gifted electronic boxes. The anomaly in work &

work-culture disappointed me the most. The job role didn't differentiate who is who. For instance, an account opening would be done by all alike, peon, clerk & officer, Depending on who is available to handle the counter. Similarly, you could be made to do the teller to do payments, generally a role assigned to clerical staff. There was no visible hierarchy. Barring the branch head, the officers were mere officers on paper, executing the same work as was done by even the attendants. This I consider a major reason encouraging the exodus of the lucky men, who somehow find an early exit.

The second anomaly was absence of any creative element in the role you played. You had little to decide over.

Just work akin to a brick maker, who has that defined mould to make the same bricks through it, over & over again. You only enter the set commands to get the work done. Nothing more, nothing less! You would get so immersed with this non-creative work that hardly one notices how fast the day passed. Add to the misery, a break spanning for just 30 minutes in between to complete your lunch & whatever else you could in this brief breather. Interestingly even this limited lunch break would commence by the time the rest of the world would be done with evening tea, at 2.00 P.M & quite naturally, by that time the hunger was already beginning to wane.

While I was now the foot soldier, forced into an unknown territory, left to fend for myself, in front of details of men in a hurry to get their business done in an unbusinesslike fashion & behind an empty looking column, my branch head called me up. Possibly having realised my curiosity to escape, he had an otherwise elaborate conversation with me in his more bright looking cabin. After asking for my educational background, he now preferred to send me in the advance section. As the area would calm my nerves, my Senior Mr. Fayaz Ahmad, an engineering graduate, would ensure, I remain nervy. He would every now & then cajole my dying spirits & encourage me to plan an exit from these terribly busy corridors. He still must be laughing loud for my helplessness.

"When The Job Robs You Off Your Creativity Inhibits Your Dynamism, Ceases Your Initiative, It Is Time To Rejig, Re-Equip, Rethink To Rediscover Yourself"

Along with sol, soul submitted !

Chapter VII

Might: The Sole Measure Of Right?

They woke us up to an eerie ugly dawn

Sly slingshot of conquer cohere

Novious vexation to lure this pawn

To falsify the name, to shame endear

Ye sharpen grimace, be dagger drawn

Beware my men this venom steer

Mayday call to this hideous plan

Tis mesh is woven , stay clear

Vitiate the design of this impure clan

Call out loud what doth appear

A vicious detract with no figurehead to warn

But for the memoirs of the dead saints we revere

Still being traded by many a moron

Who acquiesce to rally in the annals of despair

Those accomplices who brought us here

Are there to abet, don't count them gone

Their pretension to scare & swear

Is a thick trick upsleeve, so better disown

Gather ye courage to an onslaught so severe

By traitors merit abhorrence, be overthrown !

An eminent philosopher, Locke once observed,

'In the state of nature, law of nature alone is in force & every man is in his own right charged with the execution of it.' while in a civil state, law of nature is supplemented by civil law'. In the former situation, every man turns to be a judge in his own cause, while as in the later, state itself sits in judgement for him.

To judge & to be judged are two different things & true the juxtaposition of the two in the former case was believed to be violative of the notion of justice. The maxim, "nemo judex causa sua", i.e., no man can be judge in his own cause, a well established doctrine of natural justice, will not permit an individual's whimsical or self-centric approach to settle claims. To me there is an exception though, one may do as he pleases as long there is no competing claim. One easily sits in judgement for himself, for what he shall wear, drink or eat, as long he doesn't steal to wear, drink or eat. But once you stretch your arm only to find another man's nose, your inquisition process sets in, forcing you to either stop short of the ensuing hinder for the other person is also deciding his recourse simultaneously, or still proceed to endure any consequences, a rationalistic paradigm. The journey traversed from the state of nature to that of the civil state has been considered an eventual breakthrough, an outcome of a larger revolution, which shattered & shook some age-old philosophies to their very core, giving birth to certain new ones. I, however advance a note of abundant caution about getting complacent here. Revolution & the newness as a consequence must not be taken on its face value. As an ideal construct in the direction of actualisation. As we read through, what may appear a bright spot might actually turn out to be a huge disappointment.

Notwithstanding its unwarranted misuse in the contemporary era, the rise of this institution, the state, was a huge turn around in the course of history. The reason for the birth of this institution was purely two-fold in the beginning, the administration of justice & defence. Why? Because, it was felt that an organised collectivism instead of individualism shall serve the larger community purpose more effectively both in terms of advancing defence as well as serving justice. However the meaning, scope & content of this institution, kept on changing, depending upon the tending inquisition & the philosophy of the ruler, the reign & the ruled.

For instance, the Saxon ruler, Alfred, did not prevent private recourse to justice during his reign. His approach was not an absolute prohibition to private vengeance, but merely its regulation. The regulation though merely in semblance was sowing to germinate something more awful in times to come. This way the victim continued to play judge in his own case but with a semblance of regulation, which ensured the victim didn't turn into an absolute judge with unbridled powers. For instance if two men appear to threaten each other physically to prove a point, the third party would actually assist at their behest & at the most invite both to fight physically to settle scores & sit around as a referee to declare the real outcome of the contest. This would in turn attach some credibility to who was justified in walking away with the spoils, to avoid getting it called a 'grab'. In this case, the power to judge was consensually conceded to the referee. It was a bottom-up approach firmly rooted in the will of 'the contestants' in the immediate illustration. No compulsion to fall in line through a diktat. In this period in England, especially concept of "trial by a battle" took emergence. Between the claimants, a battle came to be made a legal device to settle disputes, varying from the above stated scenario in the following manner. As per this philosophy the triumphant took the spoils for the reason that victory in such cases was believed to have been facilitated by "judicium dei", i.e., the judgement of heavens to the merits of the case. The patent lacunae of these approaches would further the tempt for an alternate mechanism, which in the long run garnered momentum for a possible reform. Contrastingly in totalitarian states as in Nazi Germany, state assumed unfettered & indefinite powers of judgement, while administering the so called justice. The absolute prohibition of private recourse on one hand & the absolute exercise of whim on the other was the hallmark of such rule. Now here there obviously was no scope to contest. You were supposed to purely follow what the reign ordered & concede accordingly. This type of power to sit in judgement was acquired & not conceded. This was an extreme contrast to the previous notions. A striking blow to the will theory. This was a top-down construct, wherein the powerful makes the weaker oblige & do everything, notwithstanding one's natural drives.

This can be illustrated by a few examples, which I attempt to theorise accordingly;

a.   Systematic organised gains-

Suppose a person in your distress charms you with his sympathy & you considering him your most loyal well wisher, get so ingrained in his guidance, that you let him decide everything for you over a period. You only chance yourself with losing everything in this belief systematically perpetuated that he will do you a service.

If you innocently let him in, he may cunningly drive you out.

b.   Imposed conversional bargains-

We are born unequal! Inequity has its own rational reasons. We are bestowed with differential physical, mental & psychological standards. Here we act or get restrained from an act owing to our capacities. Now consider this scenario. A man 'A' woman 'B' are in love with each other, owing to their tested compatibilities. Naturally one would plead that they shall be blessed with a walkover to their intended marriage. Nevertheless barring luck coming to their rescue, which is purely circumstantial, they may still end up breaking. For example in the case under reference, another man 'C' falls for the same woman. He has two options to win it over. One he convinces 'b' to opt for him reading out what ifs & what nots. She may give in, if he appears more manipulative &persuasive. Or he fails, he brings in other influence, say owing to his standing. In both cases he is actually engineering a change &

manipulating things to his advantage. The scenario can get more interesting if the first man getting apprehensive of the loss, pursues resistance. An equal or unequal contest may ensue. Whoever triumphs gets emboldened to walk away with the woman. In the instant case, if 'c' is the eventual winner, it is a forcible conversional gain. Both in theatrical & actual world standards, the result will be considered 'tragic' & the gainer, despite the triumph, will still be cursed as a "villain". For whatever is induced, naturally contrasts with the original. Here he forces himself in, to ensure you are forced out of the equation.

c.   Assumed sustained generalisation-

Any reformation is not a cakewalk. The propounder is put through a lot of heat & dust. He challenges the firmly rooted status quo & revolts against an orthodox clan. Any success has to be a long & consuming affair. Now given the resistance to such change, even the eventual success is just a consolation unless the proposed change saves its author from a delusional embarrassment if its application takes things back to square one, only to search for new answers to the newly generated problem. Now in the instant case, whilst the author of the change, assumes that the change is for the larger good of the people, he continues with this vague generalisation throughout despite resistance. For example, when the Maharaja of Jammu & Kashmir acceded to India, he assumed the decision was for the larger benefit of the people of his country (J&K was a country then). It was bad in two aspects. One, he was a monarch from a minority Hindu clan & was no way delegated the power to cede territory on behalf a Muslim majority & secondly he seldom made an effort to seek suggestions from the general public. The misleading insight may possibly have come from his own person or through some random advisors having a particular mind-set which eventually may have led to outweighing & ignoring the larger dimension. This assumed generalisation that everybody will be fine with this decision since they themselves believe it to be that way, has actually turned out to be complete farce. To negate the fault lines, there is a sustained effort to legitimise the vague generalisation. Like in order to crush dissent of any kind, new measures are put in place every now & then to sustain this assumed generalisation. Again in J&K, whilst the internal strife continued, a bogus election in 1987 came to be conducted in order to legitimise what I call the "assumed sustained generalisation" & promise the state a chosen local government. The elections are widely believed to have been rigged to ensure a party complicit in the scheme, grab power, & a rogue government gets installed. By virtue of the centre could easily do as it pleased & yet escape accountability by shifting the onus on the so called elected representatives. It further put a question mark on the intention of the incumbent power, which despite a low voter turn out, instead of keeping the intended change credible, ensured it was adultered. The general populace revolted & the consequences were ominous as militancy broke out in 1989. By events like these, the credibility of any state or institution gets shaken to its very roots. The continual sustained effort since then to revive things in this direction are yet to yield any encouraging results.

Be it as may, in all cases, a contested claim was made to believe of settling things down. Throughout an invisible or a symbolic regulator in conduct is very much at play. A campaign of the sorts had long taken roots to concretise this regulatory aspect into form. Men & groups, the mighty, assuming power, exploiting the mentioned inequities proceeded to inculcate a sense that a visible third party in form will offer resolution to all ensuing problems. The abstractness in natural law came to be pleaded as a justification.

The systematic organised gain, the imposed conversional bargain & the assumed sustained generalisation, were utilized as tools for the society to slowly manipulate & entrap. To make people believe that the might will secure the right of all alike. The mighty asked for conceding the right to judgement in return for maintenance of order in the society. The problem sets in at the very outset. For a certain rule to flourish, one is made to negotiate with his freedoms. This conceding of rights for governance considered to be one progressive step is actually imbued with retrogressiveness. Although this phenomenon sought to advance justice on the one hand by empowering a third party, which got institutionalised into the modern day state to stand in judgement & deliver, yet it took the whole thing by the other, by slowly usurping untrammelled discretion bereft of any morals. The discretion as follows from the preceding discussion was an invention to do the obvious. The discretional aspect has acted as a roadblock to the real administration of justice. This thought had prompted reformists to seek a change, wherein they proposed to vest authority in someone who enjoyed public mandate, based on consensus. This paved a way to the present day democratic notion of governance doing away with the autocratic norm. Thus the government of the people, by the people & for the people became a new slogan. This measure was seen to be an instrument of change which could take care of the community as a whole & not a single individual. The 'might' as a sole measure of 'right' was discarded to facilitate the righteousness of one's claim or in other words introduced the much needed 'justness' in the administration of justice in word as well as deed.

Saint Augustine's proposition is worth to quote here, "lex ineusta non est lex", which means an unjust law is no law at all. The proposition came handy for the reformists who wanted to break the shackles of the narrow conception of justice, facilitating its incorporation in the present day law-making & law enforcing, from the substantive as well as procedural standpoint. Thus rule of law & not rule by law was supposed to prevail. The justice further was to be administered without fear or favour.

At the same time it was proposed that justice ought to be administered without passion, as when the passion comes at the door, justice flies by the window. This thesis was possible only in civilized societies, which Rawls calls the 'basic structure'. As per him the fundamental idea of a well ordered society, i.e., a society effectively regulated by public conception of justice is a companion idea used to specify the central organizing idea of a society as a system of fair co-operation . He further adds that a political society is well ordered conveys three things.

Firstly, & implied by the idea of public conception of justice, it is a society in which everyone accepts & knows that everyone else accepts, the very same political conception of justice. Moreover this knowledge is mutually recognized; people know everything they would if their acceptance of these principles were matter of public agreement. For instance the demonetization in India could turned out to be a precursor of catastrophic consequences. Since the decision is completely averse to the notion of public agreement. As majority of the population would never have voted in favour of such a radical change given the loopholes which outweigh its positive impact. Imposing a decision of such a kind inflicts pain & avoids pleasure.

The notion of arresting the circulation of black money (as intended) by this drastic measure is akin to punishing the whole for the sin committed by a few. Secondly, & implied by the idea of effective regulation of public conception of justice, society's basic structure, i.e, its main political & social institutions & the way they hang together as one system of co-operation is publicly known for good reason believed to satisfy those principles of justice. Here the system of checks & balances assumes paramount significance. Most of the modern constitutions as such insist on the system of checks & balances. If we take the example of Indian set up in consideration, we will notice the forefathers have given this conception a serious thought, making a sincere effort to separate the three vital organs viz the judiciary, legislature & executive from each other, which are co-ordinate & equal in their respective sphere. All deriving power from the constitution. But when a retired chief justice, immediately accepts a nomination on superannuation to Rajya Sabha, the fine checks & balances are thrown to the bin. Similarly when matters of public importance are stretched on & on while as individual motivated matters receive urgent hearing, the direction taken only becomes more of a hazard. This paradox was recently visible when the matters of National importance got delayed at the temple of justice while as an individual's case was heard with extreme urgency.

Thirdly, & also implied by the idea of effective regulation , citizens have normally effective sense of justice, that is one that enables them to understand & apply the publicly recognized principles of justice, & for the most part to act accordingly as their position in society, which its duties &obligations require .for instance if a person is drowning & is crying for help. A passer-by observing the same & ignoring the call for help, in most of law states would consider him not guilty as he legally may not be duty bound to protect a person other than his own self. However in societies with strong moral & religious inquisition, the same shall be considered a serious wrong & shall be considered condemnable. Thus right duty co-relation in such a case loses relevance with only 'duty' taking the centre-stage. The proposition "the only right a person has is always to do his duty", becomes a norm in such society. The orderly societies in the contemporary era ought to prefer popularity of action. Thus public opinion plays a vital role, both in the matter of declaration of rights & duties as well as enforcement of claims. The private vengeance gets transmuted into criminal justice administration while as civil justice takes the place of violent self-help. And interestingly in the case of criminal justice the law does no longer merely seek to punish the offender but in fact goes a step further by making an effort to reform the individual charged with a misdemeanour.

The conceived idea was to go a long way in ridding the system from the nuances of totalitarianism. Alas! The object has been frustrated to an extent that we are witnessing a complete reversal in the trend. The following points would sufficiently detail the reversal.

Elections: In the contemporary era, hardly do we come across an election result which is not contested later. Rigging, influence, manipulation, force, intimidation has slowly become the new normal to grab the power. Rarely a fairly contested & declared result makes for an exception. So largely I doubt this is 'by the people'

Representatives: How many times a political party seeks feedback from the voters about their choice for the representative. Tickets are issued as per the party interest to its loyals, irrespective of his acceptance. Now when similarly chosen contestants are thrown before the public, they are left with little to choose & go by an intuition.

Governance: The history leads us to conclude that state was to merely regulate things or at most govern in a good sense. But exactly opposite is done. A mandate (what they call it) is abused by enacting legislations giving enormous discretion to the governing at the cost of governed. Regulations markedly outweigh concessions.

Fine checks & balances:

The executive: Permanent executive is subordinated to temporary executive since the elected are supposed to be accountable. Notwithstanding this, the bureaucrats are made to rule for indefinite periods. Everything done by them as such becomes bad in law & this is the worst kind of abuse. Take the live example of &K, since august 2019, there is no trace of a popular government. The void is filled by empowering people who aren't accountable before the public. This only takes things back to where it had started.

The court: To avoid the abuse by the ruler, courts were established. To interpret the constitutional principles, to declare a law void if it goes against the mandate of law, to punish the guilty, to protect the rights of people enshrined in the constitution, in short to act as the eventual authority to ensure justice is not only done but seemingly appears to be done.

To be fair is to be fearless. To be called fearless, one is supposed to be impartial. And to be impartial one must be left independent. The independence of judiciary became a debate when a serving chief justice assumed a political office upon retirement which goes against the spirit of the constitution. There are many examples of glaring abuse in this context.

The media: The media is considered as the fourth pillar of democracy. A credible media will question the incumbent government on its policy lapses. In India an altogether different definition has been given to media. Most of the media in India has become a mouthpiece of the rulers, parroting out a biased version of everything.

This is a dangerous paradigm & will only degenerate the society further.

Light a candle, tighten the hook

Gleam a light beaming thy nook

Don't even bother your empty crania

Just sway down that abandoned brook

What was on offer, stands offered

Hold on thy horses, hold on this look

Be warned of these pious saints

The noblest of all remnants

Who will curse a brain tease attempt

Nonchalantly if one undertook

Chapter VIII

The right was never conceded

Rousseau, in his celebrated treatise, 'the social contract', as early as in 1762, observed & very rightly so,

"man is born free but everywhere he is in chains"

Despite so much of growth the human civilization has been through, one question still eludes every conscious citizen. Why at all does a state sit to regulate the rights of an individual, which accrue naturally, simply being born with certain inviolable, inalienable & unalterable rights. These are never concessions of any kind, by any means from any manufactured rule. But blessings for the creation from its creator. Any concession, one can think of is the one travelling from an individual towards a state as a beneficiary with the expectation that it would empower an otherwise powerless state with some semblance of regulatory authority. This cannot justify to rid the bequeathing individual with anything & everything, so as to manipulate it the other way round. This bequeathing of concession from the individual is a mere trust reposed in the hands of a small group of men & must be taken likewise to inculcate a sense of responsibility on the so called state.

The horrifying destruction witnessed during world wars woke mankind to devise certain norms to save the sacrosanctity of the human rights. Voluminous legislations have been promulgated on this aspect at every operative level. With awareness, necessitated by new age needs of survival , mankind discovered certain new rights forming an integral feature of his liveliness, recognizing them as the human rights. Generation after generation, these human rights also broadened in scope & size. And in the current context, the 'communicative rights', came to established as the fourth generation human rights, attaching the same inviolability like other predecessor human rights. Accruing to an individual plainly by due to his humanness with an intrinsic character to prevent their violation. In today's age, this right becomes the first causality in a totalitarian rule. For a state fiddles with the concession, misappropriates the trust, steals the right & colours it with the tone of protectionism. This hideous self serving pattern actually defeats the very objective of state. Who will remind the author of this manipulation that it cannot do covertly, what it cannot dare overtly. Illustrating further on the maintenance of public order, which the state pleads in its defence every now & then, the state is actually hiding behind its incapacity to govern. Here i am reminded of a wise quote, 'let 100 guilty men escape punishment but let not a single innocent individual suffer'. A sweeping & all encompassing generalisation of curbs on one's right to express has criminal overtures. If the state, armed with resources, fails to establish peace without trampling the rights of the governed as a whole, it must understand, it has got no business anymore. Any law that falls short of placing the majority populace on board, is bad in method as well as spirit. In the words of a great saint, Augustine, "lex ineusta non est lax", which means an unjust law is no law at all. Thus an enforced unjust law, may appear to be a law in letter but certainly fall flat on the touchstone of spirit. In Jammu & Kashmir, the same has promoted enormous pain & subjugated any desired pleasure! The unjustness has been orchestrated into a norm, wherein the gag is perpetuated with impunity. The restriction to express & have access to information has reduced the residents to second class citizens in their own land. Every fortnight the government will sit to judge for example on the reconsideration of allowing 4g internet access but to no utter surprises, delivers the manipulation brazenly, vowing to continue with the unjustifiable ban. The people have been left literally begging to restore the high speed internet, an otherwise sacred right. But the same falls to the deaf ears! In a mockery of the worst kind recently, the state has shamelessly concluded, in its response to numerous petitions in the Supreme Court, that right to high speed internet is not a fundamental right. It will be very interesting how the temple of justice rises to the occasion to interpret this right. Whether it will allow a broad light debauch or take a moral high ground.

To my understanding, this blanket ban is not only the violation of an established fundamental right, falling squarely in the category of fourth generation human rights but also amounts to failure of the state to protect a freedom, it never was mandated to annul. The worst addendum, I am afraid is, the perpetuation of the same in absence of a representative or popular government in the state. The application machinery is the deep state in

the form of paid executive, who exact obedience &
ensure compliance sans any accountability!

(You continue to subjugate me only to evoke more
passion & reinforce my belief. Notwithstanding your
curbs, this fearless breeze shall continue to grow flowers)

Chapter IX

The Ensuing Tragedy: Of A Fallen Hero

Prayers & prayers alone !!!

Life would be such cruel joke

For the nightmare that has woke,

Us up in cold & quite

For the one who was far ahead than us all

Who talked big & walked tall

Dominated me & dad in chess

Leaving us all spellbound& in guess

He would cut me to my size

He was blessed he was wise

Be in cricket or in maths

He would score effortlessly high

Alas! I keep asking myself, then why?

Did he lose it all, to such an inglorious fall

But then believers rely on hope

The cautious tread on a tight rope

Witnesseth the ruin of a lifetime

10 years & more, down the line

Yet his mercy, the faith dint shaken

Bear witness for the creature forsaken

Who would as a teenage boy

Early to mosque & up with joy

He still remembers your words by heart

The long holy verses, the writ, the thought

In his stills, he is still lying at your door

Seeking forgiveness to let this over

Heard you don't abandon your people in grief

Your omnipresence, inside down & deep

When cometh the blessed showers

When you wield all might & powers

& raineth washing the whole sins

For maybe the subject or kins,

Have been guilty on any count

Shall seek refuge from unending hound !

May almighty ease our pain.

Ah! What gifted batsmanship skill this gentleman was born with. Started playing during his early school days & immediately started showing signs of class & pure craft. His art gave a whole new definition to batting at a place which had little to offer on this score during those days.

The sooner the ball was delivered, the tall, apparently still &calm posture would all of a sudden come to life &as the willow in his hand swirled, in the blink of an eye, the leather would get despatched out of the eye sight. The brute power couple with that sweet timing would elude any bowler of repute. His presence at the crease was phenomenal & massive.

The physical supremacy, with strong shoulders, was just not all that met the eye. He possessed the mind of an artist with a hawkish hand-eye co-ordination, springing that treat to watch hurrying front foot, with a knee down pulsating that sweet sounding glorious cover drive. His tall reach would make him turn even good length deliveries into juicy half vollies.

As he waved the his heavy wood, a heart stopping "shoo" like sound would reverberate across the bowling end, putting the bowlers in absolute fear & awe.

In his own words, "the swirl of my bat can kill a bird flying miles away".

But as the luck would have it, the promising career was cut short with an ensuing ailment. Anything, absolutely anything can be put at stake to ensure the comeback of this magician to feast on his stroke play on field &feel the class he wore off field as well.

Chapter X

The Growth Story: Ramhall Champions League

"Daring ideas are like chessmen moved forward. They may be beaten, but they may start a winning game"
'johan wolfgang'

Self-belief converts a raw idea into something meaningful, manipulating it to become a sucessful enterprise & reach its avowed objective. The self-belief coupled with the hunger, compels one to embark on challenging missions, the very next moment of conceiving the idea.

For me the spark may lit in the dead of the night & force me towards the drawing board to workout a blue print. As a kid, despite being not so bad with the studies, i never yearned to work harder at the classroom but would save all my energy & focus for the cricket field instead. However the expectational pulls on the academic front from the well wishers, would always play a spoil sport & ruined any prospects of making it.

The distraction in focus was ostensibly not doing any good to the imposed avocation even, facilitating more mediocrity than any excellence.

To me the smell of a leather ball was a drug & believe me i was high on this drug during my school days. I fondly remember a revered teacher scolding me in classroom by saying & i quote "well you have it in you to secure excellent grades but this stupid love for this game will ruin you & i heard you sleep next to your bat these days". True, even my fantasies included competing & performing at bigger platforms rather than picking up good grades at the school.

Albeit, the dream remained elusive yet the love never died!!!

Coming to the actualisation part, the prospects (if any) were further dented by lack of any platform during those days. Though we had numerous leagues being forced on us in the pattern of village teams (100s in number) competing to reach a final (which never took place). It was more like a mafia than any competition. More dis-service than any service. With no team limits, the matches would go on & on, fee collected & the organisers disappeared in winters with traces of no return to where things were left. New threads used to be picked up & the exploit continued. Coming back to the 'platform thing' which was non existent, no stars born, no new face projected & no emergence on the scene.

But one outstanding thing about these tournaments was the intensity in contest would draw patriot crowds, men, women, young & old out on the field to support their village team.

Whilst the other areas kept producing players of repute, we got consumed in this mess with nobody taking notice of any talent. This was a huge setback for young, enthusiastic & budding players like me.

This prompted a desire for reform. But to initiate a reform, you have to either find a leader or discover one in yourself, in order to garner acceptance to the proposal of breaking the status quo.

As a school boy, that was pretty tough. Albeit the burning desire forced me to take up the challenge. The much needed experience to lead had come from being elected as captain in my village team in my early teens "Unique eleven Shaheenpora".

Learning curve from this team was over-reliance on us two brothers, Sajad & me to win a game for them. While Sajad Shayiq, my younger brother, was enjoying his batting prime during those days, i was playing second fiddle bowling at a decently steady pace & bounce. Though we kept performing in bits & pieces, but with not many match winners around, the effort would most often than not, go in vain !

In this background, i envisaged the idea of having a strong side, a well-oiled unit which could give any top notch team a run for their money.

The thought culminated in pooling in the best around to shape Ramhall cricket club (RCC) as early as in 2000, at an age when i was still in my 10th or 11th class. Taking the charge of the newly found club, i straightaway organised a league with an altogether different feel to experiment its potency. The club fared well &immediately started tasting success after success & stormed into its maiden finals. But the joy was short-lived !

As luck would have it, absolutely before the title match, some seniors ganged up & hatched a conspiracy. The ulterior motive was not to allow a teenager like me to dictate terms to them & bypass them to lift the trophy. There motive succeeded & giving no damn consideration as to what had gone into the making of this club, leaving all courtesies aside, the seniors, who i had pooled in to form this unit, dislodged me from captaincy well before the toss could take place. This was a humiliating experience & in protest i stood out of the final game. But since i was the organizer of the league also, i preferred to chew the bitter pill & conducted the first of its kind final in the area, Ramhall. Since i had pooled the best available resource, understandably the club won & registered its massive presence at the scene. The rcc was born !

Notwithstanding the skirmish, i regained the lost captaincy over a period in time. I would not be complacent anymore & to avoid any future coup to ruin the progress, we started preferring young over old & eventually finding no soft kills anymore, slowly but steadily forced the conspirators into retirement.

The idea had worked. The players eventually found at least an all inclusive Ramhall club, as the most wanted platform to express themselves in those days.

As things were in progression, a major state league was announced by J&K police by the name (ppcpl), with a maximum of 8 teams to compete. I considered this a game changing opportunity & wished to grab it with both hands. Despite an almost impossible to manage franchise fee, i nevertheless started to search for avenues. I along with a few like minded fellows requested everyone to help us with the franchise fee but it wasn't forthcoming. With no help, i conceived yet another idea of pooling money by way of player donations. We selected 8 icon players, charging 20,000 per player & then i convinced some cricket enthusiasts & like-minded fellows to help with the shortfall amount. Eventually we succeeded in participating in the high voltage event & rest is history. This league tested everyone's calibre & we gathered a fair degree of insight at the league. The hype among players fizzled out with hardly any player from Ramhall performing exceptionally. I was the only gentleman to be able to clear the ropes at sheri- kashmir stadium. Rest struggled to even find singles. The worst part of the story was i was the highest run getter from Ramhall with a modest highest score of just 23 runs. Though we won a few games, it was all due to the efforts of players from outside Ramhall. The cat was out of the bag. I now realised a lot of home work was required to create a talent pool within Ramhall so that players from within Ramhall excel & get noticed & make us proud. This led me to conceive & build upon another idea giving birth to the 'Ramhall Champions League' & with continual growth of this brand, the results are out in the open!

Today we have the desired rich pool of cricketers, who are second to none, thanks to the huge exposure & training in RCL. Now we have a platform & consequently local stars are born every day.

Chapter XI

Blessings in Disguise

Many a times, despite your upright posturing, having more to do with your carefully managed upbringing, there will be men & women who leave no stones unturned to bring you down on your knees. In their tryst to satisfy ego, or satiate their complex, or barely out of jealousy & ill will, they surpass all fine lines of decency & morality, perpetuating a modus operandi of their own kind to effectuate their smear campaign. As a victim, there are usually two options under such hostile circumstances depending upon the actual personage you exhibit. A meek man may yield or in a bid to appease may even submit. But then we must remember, people who will run after you, no matter what, shall continue to pursue their design, even if you keep ignoring their poke & prefer to move on. This attitude emboldens minions to such irreversible extent, they eventually fancy sitting on your shoulders, which in that case will only further your exploit. A reconciliation of sorts is practicable only, should you discover an element of discernible sanity over their shoulders. But once you are clear about the futility of such exercise, you must in all cases stand up & resist, to the extent of teaching such unworthy minions the lesson of their life time. In common parlance, it is absolutely doable. Though in many cases, for instance the one in mine, there are times when an open confront may expose you to high risk & less reward. I have many such experiences to unwrap but would rather stick to a few of the many episodes wherein it was all connected to my ramblings in a professional but charged environment. It was the boiling summer of 2016, when a popular rebel in valley had fallen. The whole valley was brought to a grinding halt, with almost every aspect of life including work thrown out of gear. In banking, despite all odds, we would try to keep the clientele serviced & to strike a fine balance between precaution & necessity, owing to say your managerial handicap, the management pressure or your own conscience, a few hours of work in the office in a controlled environment was inevitable. Pertinently barring banks, which chalked out modalities to keep the show going on, all other establishments were shut down like never to open again. Amidst these life threatening circumstances, we bankers would, gather courage & hurry ourselves to the work places. Whilst the new normal was in force, I was delegated with managing the business unit, some 20 kilometers away from my home, in absence of the branch manager, who had discovered a perfect time to go on a long leave. During these days, like every other commodity, even our stock in trade, the cash was scarce. We would discover our own methods to manage with such scarce resources, by setting our own limits on withdrawals for instance. One fine day, as I along with my staff, eased through a deserted market, into the premises through a makeshift entry, to escape any eventuality, in case there was one, we were welcomed with broken window panes, on the entrance, on the pavement & scattered all over the hall. On enquiry the watchman relived a horrible experience as he narrated the tale of unimaginable destruction. A stone fight had ensued the previous evening & the angry stone throwers after giving the security a tough time had vanished with no trace from the Awoora market. Out of sheer frustration, as per the witnesses, the policemen then let loose all hell, breaking whatever they caught sight of. And in the process, our bank building, which apparently was the biggest security threat to them, was invaded with stones, windows & glass broken & I still am clueless why they forgot to unfurl a flag atop, after displaying such courage & bravery. The invaded & almost conquered premises bore witness to such filthy, unprofessional & unwarranted attack that was actually enforced upon the inanimate objects by the so called law enforcers. Be it as may, & what could be even otherwise done, in such a situation, we got the mess cleared & busied with our random chores. As already said, disbursing cash in bits & pieces was the sole priority so that people would have a semblance of liquidity to sustain their bread for survival. As things were this murky, harsh tones reverberated through the hall & got more pronounced with every passing second to force me from the branch head cabin towards the hall to find out what was going on. To my utter surprise, the brave men, whose anecdote of bravery was just getting written as a memoir in the preceding paragraphs, were seen threatening our cashier to feed them with more cash than was afforded. Without any regard to the crises & instead of helping in managing the same, they were actually accentuating things further. On my intervention & trying to convince them to take whatever was being distributed, in view of the scarcity, they failed us yet again. In a sharp contrast, to my submission, they started charging towards me but finding me in no mood of a retreat, they restricted themselves to threats alone & stopped short of getting physical. The worst argument they presented was since they are tasked with maintaining law & order, they deserved a preferential treatment over the regular customers. This was so annoying given how they had enforced the law the previous evening with their bravery written all over the torn place, I couldn't stop making them realize what kind of law they were actually enforcing & instead protecting public property, they were in fact plundering the same in frustration & incompetence. I made them understand another law by declining them any cash at all. I returned their withdrawal slips with the remarks, "without passbook", & insisted upon production of the same to avail the amount we were actually disbursing. They left but not before stooping to their usual low again. By threatening to avenge, & exact that by virtue of my disappearance under the circumstance was quite a possibility.

As luck would have it, the few policemen amongst the horrible lot had some connections with the chief minister's security. Coming upto the expectations, they tried to practice the threat by using this proud network. A black & black document was channeled through them to police headquarter Srinagar & routed to our corporate headquarter. And a trial & trail of mails ensued. Phones started to ring from CHQ to zonal office to cluster office, our visible chain of bosses sprung into life. A phone call in between from the corporate headquarters from an unknown caller, who appeared to struggle with his breath as he talked to endlessly with such audacity of taking no word in return, I gathered a bit of courage & replied in the same tone & temper once he was exhausted & done with his verbal diahorrea & bluntly asked him to communicate through mail since I didn't recognize him over phone. Instead of paying heed to the advisories from foes & friends alike to soften the tone & compromise on principle, I was convinced by my satisfied conscience & dutifulness to take the whole army of internal & external bosses on, albeit armed with reasoned & factual communiques alone. Eventually, the pressure from top management was getting ugly & the zonal head would every now & then impress upon the cluster head (the immediate boss), to get me to seek an apology from the policemen, despite themselves endorsing I was not at fault, only to calm things down. I was then asked by the worthy cluster head to at least submit an apology to the superintendent of police, I was taken aback, more so because our management was in a damage control mode rather than going all out in defending their official who had just performed his duty, in far better manner than the so called 'law enforcement'. But I could very well understand the helplessness a business organization finds itself in, when we have business interests at stake. I declined to apologize. In a dramatic turnaround the long haul of communications froze all of a sudden as the written communications got escalated for perusal by the chairman. The phone rang again but this time, the tone was more polished & the temper calm. The P.A to chairman sought my willingness over phone to work at the chairman's office. Having gone through all this, who would decline the offer. I without having to apologize before the men in uniform, got catapulted at the headquarters instead. The complaint the police lodged was rightfully found by the chairman as frivolous &

motivated & turned out to be a blessing in disguise. The apex authority was a graceful, resolute man with a foresight & great understanding who couldn't see his official going down to such an ugly, impending, unjustified hound. The police deservedly met with a disappointment again but not before they were policed good enough by a commoner.

www.ingramcontent.com/pod-product-compliance
Lightning Source LLC
La Vergne TN
LVHW092023190726
843493LV00002B/567